WINSTON CHURCHILL

By Fiona Macdonald

WORLD ALMANAC® LIBRARY

Please visit our web site at: www.worldalmanaclibrary.com
For a free color catalog describing World Almanac® Library's list
of high-quality books and multimedia programs, call 1-800-848-2928 (USA)
or 1-800-387-3178 (Canada). World Almanac® Library's fax: (414) 332-3567.

Library of Congress Cataloging-in-Publication Data

Macdonald, Fiona.
    Winston Churchill / by Fiona Macdonald.
      p. cm. — (Trailblazers of the modern world)
    Includes bibliographical references and index.
    Summary: Examines the childhood, war years, political career, and personal life of the twentieth-century
British statesman, soldier, and historian.
    ISBN 0-8368-5082-3 (lib. bdg.)
    ISBN 0-8368-5242-7 (softcover)
    1. Churchill, Winston, Sir, 1874-1965—Juvenile literature. 2. Great Britain—Politics and government—
20th century—Juvenile literature. 3. Prime ministers—Great Britain—Biography—Juvenile literature.
4. World War, 1939-1945—Great Britain—Juvenile literature. [1. Churchill, Winston, Sir, 1874-1965.
2. Prime ministers.] I. Title. II. Series.
DA566.9.C5M17   2003
941.084'092—dc21
[B]
                                                        2002038044

First published in 2003 by
World Almanac® Library
330 West Olive Street, Suite 100
Milwaukee, WI 53212 USA

Copyright © 2003 by World Almanac® Library.

Project manager: Jonny Brown
Editor: JoAnn Early Macken
Design and page production: Scott M. Krall
Photo research: Diane Laska-Swanke
Indexer: Carol Roberts

Photo credits: © Bettmann/CORBIS: 5, 18 top, 21, 23 bottom, 28, 32 bottom, 34, 41 bottom; © Hulton Archive/Getty
Images: cover, 4, 6, 7 both, 8, 10, 12, 13, 15, 16, 17, 18 bottom, 20, 23 top, 24, 27, 29, 30, 32 top, 33 top, 37 top, 40,
41 top, 42, 43; © Hulton-Deutsch Collection/CORBIS: 19, 22, 25, 26, 33 bottom, 35, 37 bottom, 38

Printed in the United States of America

1 2 3 4 5 6 7 8 9 07 06 05 04 03

TABLE of CONTENTS

Words that appear in the glossary are printed in **boldface** type the first time they occur in the text.

CHAPTER 1

THE GREATEST ENGLISHMAN OF OUR TIME

Winston Churchill during a radio broadcast made to the British people from the White House in Washington, D.C., in 1943.

Winston Churchill led Britain through one of its darkest, most desperate times. But he began his life as a failure. His early school reports described him as "very bad . . . a constant trouble to every body." But he ended his career as a national hero. Most British people agreed that he was "the greatest Englishman of our time."

WARTIME LEADER

Churchill's "finest hour" came during World War II (1939–1945), when countries in Europe and beyond fought against **Nazi** Germany and its allies. Led by **fascist**, **anti-Semitic** Adolf Hitler, chancellor (chief minister) of Germany from 1933, members of the German Nazi (National Socialist) party aimed to find a "final solution" to Europe's economic and social problems by exterminating Jews, Roma (gypsies), and other ethnic minority peoples. Hitler also wished to create a "greater Germany" by invading and conquering weaker neighboring states, such as Czechoslovakia and Poland.

For several years before 1939, Churchill had warned against Hitler's dangerous plans to take control of Europe and maybe the whole world. He also criticized Hitler's fascist allies, especially Italian dictator Benito Mussolini. Many people, including British prime minister Neville Chamberlain (in power from 1937 to 1940), had dismissed Churchill's fears as exaggerated, preferring to negotiate with Hitler in an attempt to seek peace. But Churchill was proved right. In 1939, Hitler's troops invaded Poland. Hitler also signed a pact with Josef Stalin, **communist** leader of the mighty Soviet Union, agreeing to divide conquered lands between them. Faced with this open aggression, Chamberlain's government felt it had no choice. To protect freedom and democracy throughout Europe, Britain was forced to declare war.

Britain in 1939 was proud, but it was not rich. Like many other nations, its economy had not yet recovered from the serious depression of the late 1920s and 1930s. It was also not ready to fight. Compared with Germany and the Soviet Union, it had few tanks, warplanes, or battleships. Its armed men were brave and willing, but most were untrained.

In 1940, Churchill was chosen to be prime minister, replacing Chamberlain. He faced a desperate situation. All summer, German fighter planes attacked southern Britain. From September on, London, Britain's capital city, was shaken by bombing attacks every night. But Churchill's resolute, uncompromising attitude inspired the British people to survive this onslaught. His defiant remarks and gestures (he liked to be photographed giving a "V for Victory" sign) together with his rousing broadcast speeches gave them the courage to fight on and win.

A row of British Hurricane planes on a runway in England in 1940.

Winston Churchill, shown here with his wife, Clementine, on his eightieth birthday, flashes his familiar "V for Victory" sign.

Churchill was a great leader whose bravery and determination saved his country—and all Europe—from **genocidal** Nazi rule. But he was not perfect. As a young man, he was reckless, selfish, conceited—and usually in debt. He entered politics chiefly to make a name for himself and to further his own career—unlike many other men and women who aimed to serve their country or help their **constituents**. He was not a good team player, preferring to voice his own opinions and back his own judgments, however unpopular they made him. He could be disloyal and often changed his mind. Like many other powerful figures, he was sometimes stubborn, willful, abrupt, and rude. He sulked, lost his temper, and bullied his subordinates. He suffered from depression—which he called his "black dog"—and quickly became bored.

Even so, Churchill inspired enormous respect and admiration for his courage and sense of duty. Today, people around the world still honor his wartime achievements and have forgotten most of his faults.

The Greatest

In *Churchill* (Macmillan, 2001), biographer Roy Jenkins said:

I . . . put Churchill, with all his idiosyncrasies, his indulgences, his occasional childishness, but also his genius, his tenacity and his persistent ability, right or wrong, successful or unsuccessful, to be larger than life, as the greatest human being ever to occupy 10 Downing Street [that is, to be prime minister of Britain].

Winston Leonard Spencer Churchill was born on November 30, 1874. His father, Lord Randolph Churchill, was an English nobleman, and his mother was an American heiress, Jennie Jerome. Winston was their first child. He was born, prematurely and unexpectedly, just seven and a half months after they were married.

FAMOUS ANCESTORS

Winston Churchill's father, Lord Randolph Henry Spencer Churchill, around 1885.

Winston Churchill's mother, Jennie, in 1888.

Churchill came from one of the most famous families in Britain. His father was the younger son of the Duke of Marlborough, a wealthy landowner and a member of the snobbish and exclusive British upper class. The Marlboroughs were descended from brilliant army commander John Churchill (1650–1722), who won many important battles for Britain against France. He was made first Duke of Marlborough as a reward. The British public and government also paid for magnificent Blenheim Palace to be built as his home. Winston Churchill was born there, in a gloomy-looking spare bedroom, while his parents were visiting.

Churchill's mother's family was also well known. Her father, Leonard Jerome, was a New York financier with an interest in horse racing. He made his money from business deals such as founding the Coney Island Jockey Club. For

Blenheim Palace, the home of Winston Churchill's grandparents and the place where he was born.

several years, he was also part owner of the *New York Times*. Her mother, Clara Hall, was said to be one-quarter Iroquois, so Churchill believed he had a Native American heritage.

In spite of their impressive ancestry, Churchill's parents were not well thought of by people in power, though they were welcome and popular guests at social gatherings. Both were headstrong and impetuous—it was said they became engaged to be married just three days after they first met. They were also very young, inexperienced, and unreliable. When they wed, two years after their first meeting, Lord Randolph was twenty-five, and Jennie was only twenty.

Lord Randolph Churchill wanted to be famous and hoped to achieve this through a political career. His family background, together with his own enthusiasm, wit, and charm (he could be very funny), led to his being given several government posts. But he was not a successful minister. Too many of his decisions were weak, silly, and unprincipled, and he was dismissed. He died in 1895 at the age of forty-six after a long illness, having failed to fulfill his early hopes and dreams.

This failure made a deep impression on young Churchill, who was only twenty when his father died. From that time on, he felt it was his responsibility to win fame and glory so that people would once more respect the Churchill family name.

Jennie was lively, gracious, and beautiful. Admirers said she was "fascinating." But she could sometimes be cold and haughty, irresponsible, and self-indulgent. She scandalized many people by her frequent love affairs. It was rumored that her second son Jack (born in 1880, and Winston's only brother) was not her husband's child. After Lord Randolph's death, Jennie married twice more. She died in 1921 at sixty-seven.

YOUNG WINSTON

Compared with many British children, Churchill had a privileged upbringing. His parents lived in fine houses with servants to cook, clean, and care for them. He had good food, fresh air, warm clothes, books, and toys. But emotionally, he was deprived. Like most other upper-class parents, Lord Randolph and Jennie spent very little time with their children. They relied on servants to

A Difficult Childhood

These two quotations reveal young Churchill's unhappy relationship with his parents.

Description of teenage Churchill by his father, 1893:

[He lacks] *cleverness, knowledge and any capacity for settled work. He has a great talent for show-off, exaggeration, and make-believe.*

Churchill's description of his mother:

My mother . . . shone for me like the Evening Star. I loved her dearly—but at a distance.

Winston Churchill
as a young schoolboy
in 1889.

look after Churchill and his brother until it was time for them to go to boarding school when they were about eight years old. During this time, Churchill became very fond of his kindly nanny, Mrs. Everest, and continued to visit her and write to her until she died.

Churchill's school days were not happy. He was intelligent, with an inquiring mind, and had an excellent memory. His best subjects were history and English literature. He was also good at writing essays. But he was hopeless at ancient Latin and Greek and puzzled by mathematics—all were compulsory subjects, which he failed miserably. At that time, boys were beaten severely if they could not learn their lessons or misbehaved, so he was often cruelly punished. Latin and Greek were also essential for admission to a university. So when he reached the age of eighteen without university qualifications, Churchill had to look for a nonacademic career.

A MILITARY CAREER

He chose the army and enrolled at Sandhurst—England's most prestigious military college—in 1893. To his surprise, he did well there, being ranked 8 out of 150 students when he graduated the next year. He also discovered that he was good at handling horses. After a vacation, visiting the United States and Cuba, he joined a **cavalry** regiment. His mother used her wide circle of friends to find useful contacts for him, introducing him to senior officers, government officials, writers, and editors. She hoped they would help him win promotion quickly and maybe also help him if he ever left the army and looked for an alternative career.

With his regiment, the 4th Hussars, Churchill was sent to India in 1896 to join the large British army stationed there. As a young officer, Churchill had plenty of leisure time. He used it for studying—especially history and politics. He also began to write novels. Churchill did see some army action—he took part in a frontier skirmish in 1897. In spite of the danger, he enjoyed it. He also wrote about it for British and Indian newspapers. They paid him—not much, but it gave him the idea for a possible future career. He had already decided that one day he would follow in his father's footsteps and enter politics. But he needed to make money first!

Churchill stayed in the army for one more year, combining fighting with journalism. He went to Africa, where British armies also guarded empire lands. Other

Jewel in the Crown

In the late nineteenth century, the British Empire was at its height. Queen Victoria, the British monarch, ruled so many lands, all around the world, that people said "the sun never set" on empire territory. The subcontinent of India, with its rich cultural heritage and ancient religious traditions, was the "jewel" in the empire crown. Britain had ruled there since 1858, building new roads and railways, developing trade and industry, and setting up an elaborate bureaucracy to govern India's vast population. Large numbers of British troops were stationed in India to protect British colonial interests.

British troops were fighting **Dervish** (Muslim) armies in Egypt and Sudan, which were occupied by Britain but not part of the empire. In 1898, Churchill took part in a battle against Dervish warriors at Omdurman in Sudan. It was the last cavalry charge by British soldiers on horseback—a historic occasion. Churchill described his own part in the battle in dramatic terms, claiming to have killed "several—3 for certain—2 doubtful . . . without a hair of my horse or a stitch of my clothing being touched." But historians now think that his claims were exaggerated; one even describes the cavalry charge as a failure: ". . . the most futile and inefficient part of the battle was the most extravagantly praised."

Winston Churchill in South Africa around 1899.

JOURNALIST AND PRISONER

By 1899, Churchill had decided to become a full-time war correspondent. He sailed to South Africa, where yet more British soldiers were fighting—this time against rival European settlers—in the Boer War.

Churchill was eager to investigate the harsh, disease-ridden prisons—called "concentration camps" (the first use of the word)—where the Boers locked up hundreds of British settlers, including women and children. But he was captured by Boer scouts and spent his twenty-fifth birthday in prison. Eventually, he escaped and made his way through hostile territory to the

South African port of Durban. When the news of his adventures was published in British newspapers, he became a national hero—for the first time.

War correspondents working in South Africa during the Boer War in 1900. Churchill, who reported for the *Morning Post*, is in the middle row, second from the left.

CHAPTER 3

SUCCESS AND FAILURE

Churchill first ran for election to Parliament in 1899, before he went to South Africa. He was not successful, but he found the experience useful and encouraging. He worked hard at campaigning, and much to his surprise, he found that he enjoyed it. His knowledge of history, love of the English language, and experience as a journalist helped him compose excellent speeches. His passion for talking (especially about himself), his curiosity, and his hunger for fresh experiences made it easy and interesting for him to meet new people and explore unknown towns.

Churchill was not an eye-catching candidate, being short, slight, and prematurely balding with wispy pale red hair. He spoke with an upper-class accent (which suggested trustworthiness and authority but also annoyed some left-wing voters) and had a slight lisp. But he was full of self-confidence, writing to a friend that "I personally have made a vy [very] good impression" on the voters and local party leaders. His youthful drive and energy and impish sense of humor also attracted attention. He felt sure that one day before long he would become a **Member of Parliament**.

MEMBER OF PARLIAMENT

Churchill soon got his opportunity to run for Parliament again. He campaigned for the Conservative (traditionalist, **right wing**) Party in the 1901 General Election and was chosen by the voters of Oldham, a northern industrial town. He understood very little about their

Two Houses

"M.P." is a short way of saying "**Member of Parliament**." Like today, when Churchill was young the British Parliament was made up of two chambers, the House of Commons and the House of Lords. M.P.s (members of the House of Commons) were elected at least once every five years. They played a vital part in government, suggesting and debating proposed new laws and voting on whether to accept them. Members of the House of Lords were not elected but had the right to share in government because of their noble birth or because they were top judges (known as "law lords") or senior bishops in the Church of England. Like the Commons, the House of Lords could vote on proposed legislation and debate new laws. (After 1911, however, the Lords could not veto laws approved by the House of Commons but could send them back there for revision.)

lives. But now, for the first time, he had power.

Once in Parliament, Churchill soon made his views known. As a backbencher (junior member), he was expected to remain silent—or meekly agree with party leaders—but that was not his style. In 1902, he criticized his own party leaders over their plans to reorganize the army. He even discussed, with other MPs, the possibility of forming a new center party. They wanted to end party squabbling and form a government that would help everyone in Britain.

In 1904, Churchill resigned from the Conservatives after disagreeing with them once more on economic policy. In 1906, he ran for election as an M.P. again. This time, he represented the Liberal (progressive, moderate left) Party. He shared many Liberal views, but he also recognized that the **Liberal Party** was becoming

Thirty-year-old Winston Churchill as a Member of Parliament.

First Impression

Social reformer Beatrice Webb described Winston Churchill as a young politician in 1903.

Went to dinner with Winston Churchill. First impression: restless, almost intolerably so . . . egotistical, bumptious, shallow-minded and reactionary, but with a certain personal magnetism, great pluck and some originality, not of intellect but of character. . . . But I dare say he has a better side . . . his pluck, courage, resourcefulness, and great tradition [ancestry] *may carry him far.*

Liberal Party leader Herbert Asquith was an early supporter of Churchill's political career.

stronger and more popular, while the **Conservative Party** was in decline. Electors in Manchester (another northern industrial city) voted him into the House of Commons, where Liberal Party leaders welcomed him and gave him junior jobs in government. Meanwhile, the Conservatives loathed him and tried to block his career. They said he was disloyal and a traitor.

Churchill was not dismayed and remained confident that he would one day have a brilliant career. "We are all worms. But I do believe that I am a glow-worm," he declared. In 1908, he was elected to Parliament for the third time, representing the rough, tough Scottish port of Dundee. He still supported the Liberal party. Liberal leader Herbert Asquith made him a member of his government, giving him a very responsible position at the Board of Trade, a government department with important economic responsibilities. Asquith was probably the first politician to recognize

Churchill's great potential and supported him for the rest of his career. In his new job, Churchill worked closely with charismatic Welsh politician David Lloyd George. Together they shaped plans for a whole new system of state welfare benefits designed to help ordinary people who were old, sick, or unemployed. They set up labor exchanges where unemployed men and women could look for work. They introduced unemployment insurance schemes and a basic old-age pension and improved workers' rights to a minimum wage and maximum weekly working hours.

A PARTNER FOR LIFE

Churchill's political career had started well. He was also very happy in his private life. In 1908, he married Clementine Hozier, a poor relative of a Scottish noble family. "Clemmie" (as Churchill called her) was determined, dignified, and sympathetic. With tremendous tact and loyalty, she supported Churchill through all the successes and failures of his life. She dared to tell him the truth when everyone else was scared to speak out and to warn him when she thought he was behaving badly. Although occasionally they quarreled, they remained devoted to each other for almost fifty-six years. She called Churchill "pig" or "pug" (cartoonists

Welsh Liberal politician David Lloyd George, who worked with Churchill and later became prime minister.

Speechless

Clementine Hozier, Churchill's devoted wife, described her first meeting with Churchill:

. . . he never uttered a word . . . he never asked me for a dance, he never asked me to have supper with him—he just stood and stared.

later drew him as a bulldog); he called her "Clemmie-cat." They had five children: Mary, Sarah, Randolph, Marigold, and Diana. Tragically, Marigold died young.

Winston Churchill and Clementine Hozier a week before their wedding in 1908.

Churchill's next government post, in 1910, was as Home Secretary (chief minister at the Department of Justice)—a very senior job for someone so young (thirty-six). Here, he was responsible for government policy on many of the most controversial topics of the day, including workers' rights and women's right to vote. Although he was willing to listen to peaceful arguments from protesters, Churchill took a firm line against any campaigners who broke the law. For example, in 1910, there were violent riots by workers in the Welsh mining

Winston Churchill (second from right) strolling in 1910 London with David Lloyd George (second from left), Margaret Lloyd George, and a parliamentary aide.

town of Tonypandy. They were complaining about a new wage deal, which they felt was unfair. Churchill sent in troops to end the protests and restore peace. Some British people supported what he had done, but many thought he had overreacted. They said he was impatient and unwise. The next year, Churchill lost his job.

BUILDING UP THE NAVY

Churchill was not easily discouraged, and Prime Minister Asquith still believed in him. So in 1911, Churchill was given a new government appointment, as First Lord of the Admiralty (overseer of the navy). For many years, Churchill had complained that governments spent too much money on the armed forces, but now, right away—and without any embarrassment—he changed his mind. He demanded large sums to build new warships and buy weapons and ammunition. He commissioned new oil-burning ships to replace coal-fired ones, created a new naval air service, and pioneered the development of tanks.

Churchill feared, though he could not be sure, that these **armaments** would soon be badly needed. He was proved right. From 1914–1918, the nations of Europe and their allies in Russia, Australia, New Zealand, Africa, Canada, and the United States fought a terrible war in which many millions of men died. Most of the fighting took place on land, but Britain, as an island, relied heavily on warships to defend its coasts. Germany and Britain both set up naval **blockades** (constant warship patrols) to try to drive each other out of the North Sea. Gunboats also guarded other ships bringing food and essential supplies and carrying soldiers to fight on the European mainland.

Winston Churchill, First Lord of the Admiralty, speaking in 1916 to munitions workers during World War I.

At first, British army commanders were confident that the war would "be over by Christmas" 1914. But this did not happen. Instead, armies on both sides became bogged down in muddy trenches in Belgium and France. Many warships were sunk and sailors drowned. With typical impatience, Churchill put forward a daring but risky plan. In 1915, he suggested that Britain and its allies should send an attacking force to the Dardanelles, on the coast of Turkey. The aim was to help Russia, Britain's ally, attack Germany from the east. Russia could not do this in the early years of the war because it had to defend its southern frontier against Turkey, which was Germany's ally.

But Churchill's plan went disastrously wrong. Over 250,000 British and allied soldiers died. Many were volunteers from British Empire lands, chiefly Australia and New Zealand. They were shot by Turkish snipers as they struggled to wade ashore or killed by diseases carried in polluted water supplies. Before long, the whole invading army was forced to retreat. Churchill was dismissed from his job at the Admiralty and given a very junior government post instead. Shocked, saddened, and humiliated by his failure, he resigned.

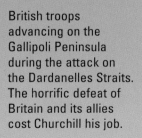

British troops advancing on the Gallipoli Peninsula during the attack on the Dardanelles Straits. The horrific defeat of Britain and its allies cost Churchill his job.

CHAPTER 4

WAR AND PEACE

Churchill could not stay idle for long. He took up painting as a hobby, but although he had real artistic talent, making pictures was not enough to satisfy his active mind. He needed to rebuild his self-esteem, which had been badly damaged by the Dardanelles disaster, and to restore his political reputation. So he volunteered to fight as a soldier on the battlefields of World War I. Because of his family background, former army service in India, and experience as a government minister, he was given officer rank. In November 1915, he was sent to fight in France.

Churchill liked being a soldier. And he was good at it. Very soon, he was promoted to Lieutenant Colonel, in charge of a large number of men. One of his senior officers wrote: "I am fairly convinced that no more

British troops in the sand-bagged trenches of France during World War I.

Front Line Warfare

Conditions at the front line, the narrow strip of land in Belgium and northern France where the two enemy armies met face to face, were often appalling. Soldiers took cover in deep trenches protected by barbed wire as sniper bullets whizzed close by, deadly shells exploded overhead, and in the later years of the war, clouds of poison gas swirled around. The trenches were dug in soft, muddy ground, which often became waterlogged. There were rats and lice, and after an enemy attack, dead bodies lay everywhere.

popular officer ever commanded troops." To encourage his soldiers in the terrible conditions of the front line, Churchill often joked, "War is a game to be played with a smiling face."

Impressive Qualities

A fellow officer describes Churchill's skills as a soldier:

As a soldier, he was hard-working, persevering and thorough.... He...[set] out to work at tiresome but indispensable details and to make his unit efficient in the very highest possible degree. I say nothing of his tactical and strategic ability—they were not tested...but I cannot conceive that exceptionally creative and fertile brain failing in any sphere of human activity to which it was applied.

Winston Churchill with officers of the French army in 1916.

Churchill shared these conditions with his men, but only occasionally. As an officer, he spent most of his time in comparative safety, making plans, writing reports, and holding meetings "behind the lines." The British army used deserted buildings—from farmhouses to castles—as operations centers during the war. Some were luxurious. Even when it was Churchill's turn to go to the trenches, he tried to make the experience as comfortable as possible. He wrote home to Clemmie, asking her to send a sheepskin sleeping bag, clean face towels, a periscope (for looking over the top of the trench in safety), thigh-high waterproof boots—and some brandy!

Churchill spent just five and a half months in France before being called back to Britain to take part in government once again. In 1916, his former colleague,

Liberal leader David Lloyd George, asked him to be Minister for Munitions (weapons). Churchill kept this job until the end of the war and helped to organize, very efficiently, the army's return to Britain from France after peace had been declared.

PROGRESS AND CONTROVERSY

In 1919, Churchill was promoted to Secretary of State for War and Air—a new job that recognized the important part that aircraft might play in future battles. Planes had been used by both sides during World War I, mostly for reconnaissance, although German air ace Manfred von Richthofen had shown the fighting potential of aircraft by shooting down eighty British and allied planes single-handedly. In 1917, Churchill wrote describing the possibilities for air warfare: ". . . the air is free and open. There are no entrenchments there. It is equal for the attack and for the defence. It is equal for all comers." With typical enthusiasm and reckless bravery, he also learned to be a pilot himself.

So far, all seemed to be going well. But then Churchill became involved with another controversial cause that threatened to wreck his political career once again. He supported a group of White Russian (conservative royalist) generals who were fighting against Bolsheviks (communist **revolutionaries**) in Russia. In 1917, communists had taken control of Russia and deposed the Czar. Many ordinary Russian people supported them. The White Russians were a small, unelected minority who were fighting to bring back the Czar. Europe felt exhausted at the end of a terrible conflict in which 10 million men had

Bolshevik leaders Josef Stalin (*right*) and Leon Trotsky on a podium in Moscow's Red Square in front of a huge crowd during the 1917 Russian Revolution, which gave birth to the Soviet union. During World War II, Stalin was the leader of the Soviet Union, which became an unlikely ally of Churchill's Britain in the fight against Nazi Germany.

been killed and a further 20 million were injured. No one in Britain wanted to get involved in another war. But Churchill continued to urge action against the Bolsheviks. This unpopular campaign marked the beginning of a deep dislike of **communism** that remained with him for the rest of his life.

In 1921–1922, Churchill was made Secretary of State for Colonies. He went on diplomatic missions to the Middle East, helping to set up new Arab states there after the collapse of Turkish power during World War I.

(For hundreds of years before 1914, the Turks had ruled a large empire there.) Churchill also supported calls from Jews to set up their own independent Middle Eastern state. In 1917, at the height of World War I, Churchill's government colleague, Foreign Secretary A. J. Balfour, had issued a "Declaration" promising a Jewish homeland in Palestine. Back in Europe, Churchill also took part in government negotiations with Irish Nationalists, who were campaigning for independence from British rule and the creation of an Irish Free State. This made him unpopular with many British people, especially the Conservatives.

Delegates to a conference in Cairo, Egypt, from a group organized by Winston Churchill to discuss the future of Arab nations.

A BREAK FROM POLITICS

But then the situation changed. Churchill started 1922 as an international statesman but ended it without a job. There was a General Election, and he failed to persuade the voters of Dundee to choose him as their M.P. This was not entirely his fault. He fell ill with appendicitis and so could not campaign. Clemmie loyally went to Dundee and made speeches on his behalf—but angry workers spat at her because they were poor, cold, and hungry, and she was wearing a valuable necklace of pearls. But even Churchill's brilliant way with words might not have gotten him elected. For several years, a new **socialist** party—the **Labor Party**—had been gaining support in industrial towns like Dundee, and the Liberals had been losing support.

For two years, Churchill was out of politics. He kept himself busy writing a volume of memoirs called *The World Crisis*. Sensing that the Liberal Party was about to collapse, he also tried, once again, to start a new center political party that would be moderate but anti-socialist. But he failed. Then, in 1924, he made a dramatic switch of political loyalties, the second in his career. He left the Liberal Party and rejoined the Conservatives. He believed they would be the best party to lead the fight against socialism. He also wanted another chance to share in political power.

Winston Churchill speaking in 1924, when he was Chancellor of the Exchequer.

Stanley Baldwin, the Conservative leader, welcomed Churchill to his party, though many ordinary M.P.s and Conservative supporters were not pleased. To Churchill's surprise, Baldwin made him Chancellor of the Exchequer—head of the government finance ministry. But Churchill was not an economist—and Britain really needed an expert to manage the economic crisis that was approaching fast.

UNFORTUNATE DECISION

Churchill made a bad situation worse by his decision in 1925 to return British currency to the "**gold standard**"—that is, guaranteeing to exchange coins or pounds for their value in real gold. (The gold standard had been suspended during World War I.) This made British goods expensive on the world market and slowed

The Cost of War

It had been very expensive to fight World War I. After it ended, many factories had closed because there was no need for warships, weapons, aircraft, or ammunition in peacetime. Demand for iron, steel, and coal fell, too. There was widespread unemployment in British mining and manufacturing regions. By 1925, one and a half million men were looking for jobs. Even when people could find work, wages were so low that they could not feed their families. Men and women from the most depressed areas took part in **"hunger marches"** to London. In 1926, there was a nine-day General Strike. Although Churchill claimed to have some sympathy with the protesters, he supported the government's firm action to break the strike.

A group of women protesting against the General Strike in 1926.

down British trade. Historians have suggested that Churchill made his decision partly for romantic, not economic, reasons—he wanted to go back to the "great days" of Britain's past. But—although Churchill did not know it—worse was to come. He remained Chancellor of the Exchequer until 1929, but then the Conservative government collapsed. Churchill was still in Parliament, but he was out of power.

CHAPTER 5

THE WILDERNESS YEARS

Churchill remained out of office for the next ten years, from 1929 to 1939. Later, he was to call them his "wilderness years." For the first time in his life, he seemed lost, with no clear path to follow. Most of his political friends seemed to have deserted him. His chief political guide and protector, Herbert Asquith, died in 1928. David Lloyd George, Churchill's other old, trusted colleague, was seriously ill and retired from politics in 1931.

Winston Churchill with Prime Minister Stanley Baldwin in London before the Miners' Strike Conference of 1925. By 1930, Churchill and Baldwin had become political rivals, principally over the issue of independence for India.

CLINGING TO THE PAST

In 1929, Churchill hoped that he might be chosen to replace Stanley Baldwin as leader of the Conservatives, but senior party members did not like him or trust him. Then, in 1930, he quarreled openly with Baldwin over the question of independence for India. By 1930, almost everyone agreed that the great days of the British Empire were over. Britain was not as rich or powerful as it once had been, and many people all around the world were questioning the right of European nations to rule so much foreign land. Baldwin believed that Britain should gradually let India run its own government and make plans for its own future. The Viceroy (the king's representative and chief British official in India) agreed.

But Churchill thought differently. He believed that India should remain a British possession, and he made extremely rude, racist remarks about the Indian leader, Mahatma ("Great Soul") Gandhi, who was leading popular, nonviolent demonstrations in India to demand an end to British rule.

Indian leader Mahatma Gandhi (*center*) during a tour of Britain in 1931. Gandhi, who inspired much of the world with his nonviolent campaign for an end to British rule in India, was often the object of Churchill's scorn.

Although many people, including experts on Indian affairs, challenged Churchill's views, he refused to change his mind. This stubbornness finally ended any chance he might have had of winning back Conservative support. It angered other politicians, too. In 1931, Conservatives, Liberals, and Labor Party leaders agreed to form a National Government. They put aside their differences to work together for the good of the country—but they did not invite Churchill to join.

Tactless

Churchill made many insulting comments about campaigners for Indian independence, like this:

It is alarming and nauseating to see Mr. Gandhi . . . now posing as a fakir [holy man] *of a type well known in the East, striding half-naked up the steps of the Vice-regal* [Viceroy's] *palace . . . to parley* [negotiate] *on equal terms with the representative of the king-emperor.*

The National Government

The 1931 National Government was formed to cope with an urgent economic crisis, caused partly by the U.S. Wall Street crash of 1929, when share prices slumped and thousands of investors lost all their money, and partly by Churchill's own policy of returning Britain to the gold standard. Both led to a long economic depression—even worse than in the 1920s—with falling profits, bankrupt businesses, low wages, and widespread unemployment. By 1933, three out of every ten British workers were unemployed. The National Government cut spending on all public projects, from schools to the armed forces. It also introduced a means test, an examination of a person's financial state, to restrict welfare benefits to the most needy British people. Economic conditions slowly improved, but the crisis continued until 1939.

National Government cabinet ministers in 1931.

The National Government also faced serious political problems. These included the abdication of King Edward VIII in 1936. The king's love affair with Wallis Simpson, a divorced American woman, scandalized British people with traditional social and political views, and the British government made him choose to give up either Mrs. Simpson or his throne. (Churchill, who greatly appreciated his own happy marriage, suggested that Edward VIII should be allowed to marry and remain king as well.) The government's problems also included the rise of radical and extremist political parties. On the left, communists hoped to start a revolution and make Britain a workers' state like the Soviet union. On the right, fascists admired European leaders like Germany's Adolf Hitler and shared many of his political ideals, including state control of people's lives and anti-Semitism.

Churchill occupied his time in the political "wilderness" by writing a great deal. His books included a four-volume history of his warrior ancestor, the first Duke of Marlborough; an autobiography, *My Early Life*; a massive history of Britain; a collection of short biographies; and a book describing his own thoughts and adventures. He also wrote many newspaper articles. This writing provided him with money to live on and kept his name in the public eye, but it was not what he really wanted from life.

A Powerful Contributor

A letter to Churchill from newspaper proprietor Sir Elmsley Carr in 1937 gave positive feedback on Churchill's journalism:

Hearty congratulations on this week's article. It is, I think, one of the most interesting so far as our general readers are concerned.

Today our circulation exceeds four million net, and it requires no imagination on your part to realise what an enormous public—probably the largest in the world—you are addressing. . . .

I cannot say how delighted we are to have you as our chief contributor.

LOOKING AHEAD

Although very busy with his writing, Churchill did not give up his interest in politics. He was the first leading British politician to take the fascist threat seriously. As early as 1933, when Hitler first became chancellor (political leader) of Germany, Churchill warned of the "odious [hateful] conditions" that Hitler and his **Nazi** Party were creating there. By 1936, Churchill was stridently condemning Britain's National Government and warning that there might soon be war:

German dictator Adolf Hitler (in car) and his deputy Rudolf Hess at a Nazi Party parade before World War II.

"We cannot look back with much pleasure on our foreign policy in the past five years. They have been disastrous years. . . . We have seen the most depressing and alarming changes in the outlook of mankind which have ever taken place."

Even so, most British politicians refused to heed Churchill's warnings, hoping to avoid war by making friends with fascist governments and ignoring many of their unpleasant actions, such as taking over small, weak, neighboring countries or persecuting minority groups. This policy became known as "appeasement." Some said politicians who supported appeasement were genuinely trying to persuade the fascists to obey international law; others said those politicians were simply weak and scared. Today, some historians think that "appeasing" politicians might have been "buying time" with their policies to allow British armed forces to begin to prepare for war.

A TEMPORARY PEACE

In 1938, British Prime Minister Neville Chamberlain flew to Munich, Germany, to sign an agreement with

Leaders at the 1938 conference where the Munich Agreement was signed, settling a dispute between Germany and Czechoslovakia. British prime minister Neville Chamberlain is on the left; German chancellor Adolf Hitler is in the center.

Hitler. He returned home as a hero, claiming that he had secured "peace in our time." But less than six months later, Hitler broke the Munich Agreement by invading Czechoslovakia. Appeasement had not worked. Hitler clearly had plans to conquer Europe, and Britain urgently needed to prepare for war.

Britain declared war on Germany in September 1939. Chamberlain immediately asked Churchill to come back into government once again, as First Lord of the Admiralty. The British navy was delighted and sent a joyful signal to all the ships in its fleet: "Winston is back!"

The first months of the war did not go well. At the end of April 1940, Chamberlain and all his government were forced to resign after a planned British and French invasion of Norway failed disastrously. Who could lead Britain now?

CHAPTER 6

FINEST HOUR

Churchill became Prime Minister on May 10, 1940. For the next five years, he led Britain and its allies in a heroic struggle. As one historian has written, "his life and career became one with Britain's story and its survival." The situation was grim. And because of the 1930s economic crisis and Chamberlain's policy of appeasement, the country was not really ready for war.

GERMAN INVADERS

Yet something had to be done! German troops were advancing through Europe. In 1938, they had forcibly joined Austria to Germany and invaded Czechoslovakia. In 1939, they invaded Poland. In 1940, they occupied Norway, Belgium, the Netherlands, and over half of France. The same year, the Soviet Union, Germany's ally at that time, attacked Finland and occupied the Baltic States. Italy, another German ally, declared war on Britain and France. Hungary, Romania, Bulgaria, and Slovakia joined the German Axis alliance.

In 1940, Hitler planned to invade Britain. In early summer, German troops marched through Belgium and into northern France. (The distance across the English Channel between France and Britain is only about 20 miles (32 kilometers) at that point.) Over 200,000 British troops who had

The Nazi shelling of Dunkirk, France, the scene of the remarkable rescue of trapped British troops by thousands of their countrymen sailing across the English Channel in every sort of boat imaginable.

been sent to fight against the Germans, plus 100,000 French and Belgians, were forced to retreat. They were trapped on the beaches close to the French port of Dunkirk and had to be rescued by an extraordinary collection of ships, from rowing boats to battle cruisers. Many of the rescuers were volunteers.

High Stakes

Churchill spoke to the House of Commons on June 18, 1940, the day after Germany took control of France.

The battle for France is over. I expect the battle of Britain is about to begin. Upon this battle depends the survival of Christian civilization. Upon this battle depends our own British life and the long continuity of our institutions and our empire. The whole fury and might of the enemy must very soon be turned on us. Hitler knows that he will have to break us in this island or lose the war. If we can stand up to him all Europe may be free . . . but if we fail, then the whole world, including the United States, and all that we have known and cared for, will sink into the abyss of a new dark age.

German bombers over London in 1940.

In July 1940, German fighter planes attacked southern England and were only driven away by the astonishing bravery of British pilots who attacked German planes in aerial dogfights. These pilots were inexperienced and had only a bare minimum of training—there was no time for more.

Most were under twenty-five, and many died. In just three months (July to September 1940), Britain lost 900 planes and their crews. Churchill praised the pilots' courage and self-sacrifice in one of his most famous speeches. "Never in the field of human conflict," he declared, "has so much been owed by so many to so few."

Next, waves of German planes launched day and night raids on London and other targets like airfields and docks. These raids were at their worst from September 1940 to May 1941, but they lasted until 1945. From 1944, there were also raids by rocket-propelled "V-bombs." These raids were nicknamed the "Blitz" from the German word *Blitzkrieg*, or "Lightning War."

Killing Civilians

World War II was the first time in world history that air power was deliberately used to attack civilian populations, by both sides. Historians estimate that a total of 30 million civilians were killed in the six years of fighting, in addition to the approximately 6 million Jews who perished in the Holocaust.

Churchill's government organized defensive measures against the Blitz, such as the blackout, a ban on all visible lights after dark, and built air-raid shelters underground. It also encouraged British scientists to develop new military technology, especially radar. By 1940, it had stockpiled 1.25 million cardboard coffins and issued 38 million air-filtering masks to protect civilians from poison gas attack. But the bombing raids caused immense loss of life and tremendous damage to houses, factories, roads, railways, and docks. Over 23,000 British people were killed in 1940, the first year of the Blitz, and one-third of London was destroyed.

Winston Churchill inspecting bomb damage at Buckingham Palace in London with King George VI and Queen Elizabeth II in 1940.

INSPIRATION

Throughout the Blitz, Churchill worked tirelessly to support and encourage the British people. He traveled around the country, meeting men and women workers and praising all they were doing for "the war effort." He was over seventy years old by then but still full of energy. His visits made a great impression on all who met him, but his wartime speeches had an even greater impact. He wrote them himself and read them (often live) for broadcast by radio. They were heard by almost

An extraordinary image of life going on amid the horrors of war: a milkman delivers milk in a rubble-filled London street in 1940.

the whole British population and transmitted to British Empire lands all around the world. They were proud, defiant, rousing, and reassuring, all at the same time: "Let us therefore brace ourselves to our duties, and so bear [behave] ourselves that, if the British Empire . . . lasts for a thousand years, men will say: 'This was their finest hour.'"

Throughout 1940, Hitler made offers of peace—if Britain would give up fighting. But Churchill stayed resolute. In another famous speech, he thundered: "We shall defend our island, whatever the cost may be. We shall fight on the beaches, we shall fight on the landing grounds, we shall fight in the fields and in the streets, we shall fight in the hills; we shall never surrender."

IN SEARCH OF ALLIES

So far, Churchill—and Britain—had fought alone, with just a little help from Europeans who had managed to escape from German-occupied lands. French soldier and politician Charles de Gaulle organized a Free French army from bases in Britain; Polish, Czech, and other

East European airmen volunteered to serve in Britain's Royal Air Force. Troops from former British Empire lands such as Canada, Australia, and New Zealand also volunteered.

All this was very welcome, but Churchill knew he must find powerful allies to win the war. He began an exhausting program of "personal diplomacy," traveling long distances in difficult and dangerous conditions to meetings where he could use his wit, intelligence, and charm to persuade the two most powerful men in the world (apart from Hitler) to join in the fight to defeat Germany. These men were Josef Stalin, communist ruler of the Soviet Union, and Franklin Delano Roosevelt, president of the United States. Churchill described Roosevelt as Britain's "best friend."

The United States had already helped Britain. In 1940, Roosevelt sent guns to replace the weapons lost by retreating troops in the Dunkirk expedition. He also lent warships to help the British navy attack lands around the Mediterranean Sea that were controlled by Germany's ally, Italy. (Churchill launched a typically bold and risky attack there to weaken and embarrass Hitler.)

Roosevelt was also willing to help Britain politically. In August 1941, he met Churchill on board the U.S. warship USS *Augusta* and signed the Atlantic Charter, a rousing declaration of democratic principles that their two nations shared, containing a commitment to defend

Victory at All Costs

Churchill spoke to the House of Commons on May 13, 1940.

I have nothing to offer but blood, toil, tears and sweat. We have before us an ordeal of the most grievous kind. . . . You ask, what is our policy? I will say: It is to wage war, by sea, land and air, with all our might and with all the strength that God can give us: to wage war against a monstrous tyranny, never surpassed in the dark, lamentable catalogue of human crime. . . . You ask, what is our aim? I can answer in one word: It is Victory, victory at all costs, victory in spite of all terror, victory, however long and hard the road may be; for without victory, there is no survival.

the "free world." But Roosevelt was reluctant to send U.S. soldiers to fight in Europe or elsewhere—even though Churchill pleaded, in a radio broadcast to the United States in 1941, "Give us the tools, and we will finish the job."

Ever since the 1930s, Roosevelt had followed a policy of "flexible neutrality." It was not until Japan, Germany's ally, bombed U.S. warships anchored at Pearl Harbor, Hawaii, in December 1941 that the United States joined in Churchill's war.

Until 1941, Stalin's Soviet Union had been a close ally of Germany. In 1939, the two nations had made a pact to divide conquered lands in Eastern Europe between them. But in 1941, Hitler broke this agreement and invaded the Soviet Union, ordering his troops to march on the capital, Moscow. Stalin was furious, and Churchill saw his chance to win a new ally. He was still fiercely opposed to communism and distrusted Stalin personally. But he persuaded Stalin to fight on Britain's side. These two powerful allies made all the difference to Britain's future—and the future of the whole world.

Securing U.S. and Soviet help and friendship was one of Churchill's most important contributions to winning the war.

He was grateful—and relieved—that his "personal diplomacy" had worked: "We must all thank God that we have been allowed . . . to play a part in making these days memorable in the history of our race."

The "Big Three," (*left to right*) Soviet marshal Josef Stalin, U.S. president Franklin Delano Roosevelt, and British prime minister Winston Churchill, meet in 1943 in Teheran, Iran, to discuss allied war efforts and their countries' postwar plans.

FADING AWAY

World War II ended in 1945 after the United States dropped the first atom bombs on the Japanese cities of Hiroshima and Nagasaki. By that time, however, Churchill was no longer in power. There had been a general election in Britain earlier that year, and Churchill's wartime government had been defeated. The voters chose a Labor (socialist) government in its place.

Most British people said that they had not voted against Churchill as a man. They still deeply admired his courage and were enormously grateful for all he had done during the war. But they did not like his political views, which were out of touch with modern times. They wanted a government that would help ordinary people improve their lives and their opportunities, and that did not look back—as Churchill did—to the traditional, unequal British society of long ago.

Winston Churchill joins members of the Royal Family on the balcony of Buckingham Palace during VE (Victory in Europe) Day celebrations in 1945. Princess Elizabeth (*far left*) would become Queen Elizabeth II in 1952.

Now out of politics, Winston Churchill paints at his easel in 1946.

STILL DETERMINED

Churchill was hurt, but he would not resign. He remained an MP and began writing and painting once again. He con-

tinued to make speeches in Britain, Europe, and the United States. His most famous was on a topic that had concerned him since 1917—the growth of communist power. In 1946, in Fulton, Missouri, he warned that "an Iron Curtain is falling across Europe," dividing free democracies from communist-controlled lands. After the war ended in 1945, Soviet leader Stalin had seized control of many formerly free states bordering Soviet lands and had placed strict controls on the lives of

A Final Joke

Although old, ill, and tired, Churchill did not lose his wicked sense of humor. Shortly before he died, he joked:

I am ready to meet my Maker, whether my Maker is prepared for the ordeal of meeting me is another matter.

people living there. Correctly, Churchill also recognized that the next worldwide conflict, the Cold War, would be between two great "superpowers," the Soviet Union and the United States.

Sir Winston Churchill's funeral at St. Paul's Cathedral in London.

In 1951, when Churchill was seventy-seven, the Labor government lost power, and Churchill became prime minister again. In many ways, this was a mistake. He was now ill as well as old, and the task was almost too much for him. But Churchill remained as determined as ever and relied on willpower to survive. His last major speech (in 1955) ended with a typically brave, defiant flourish: ". . . never flinch, never weary, never despair." Churchill resigned as prime minister when he became eighty but continued as an M.P. until 1964, the year before he died.

FAME AND GLORY

Toward the end of his life, Churchill received many honors. In 1946, King George VI made him a Companion of Honour—a very rare distinction given only to men or women whom the king himself wanted to praise. In 1953, the new, young Queen Elizabeth II of England made him a Knight. From then on, he was known as Sir Winston Churchill. He won the Nobel Prize for literature in 1953 and the Charlemagne Prize, for his contribution to European peace, in 1955.

Sir Winston and Lady Churchill outside their home in 1961.

Churchill was also made an honorary U.S. citizen in 1963. This pleased him tremendously. Half American by birth, he was always eager to strengthen the links between the people of Britain and the United States. When he died in 1965 at the age of ninety, he was given a State funeral—a rare but fitting tribute to a great man.

Churchill was an extraordinary human being. He had many faults and made many mistakes in his long political career. But he was also a true national hero. By his courage and determination, he saved his country and changed the history of the world.

TIMELINE

1874	Winston Churchill is born on November 30 at Blenheim Palace in England.
1896	Serves with British army in India.
1899	Travels to South Africa as newspaper war correspondent.
1901	Elected as Member of Parliament for the Conservative Party.
1904	Leaves Conservatives to join Liberal Party.
1908	Becomes government minister, helping introduce new system of welfare benefits.
1908	Marries Clementine Hozier.
1911	Appointed First Lord of the Admiralty. Prepares British navy for war.
1915	Organizes disastrous Dardanelles invasion. After it fails, he is demoted, then resigns.
1915	Serves with British Army at front line of World War I battlefields in France.
1916	Appointed Secretary of State for Munitions (weapons).
1922	Loses seat at General election.
1924	Leaves Liberal Party and rejoins Conservatives. Reelected to Parliament.
1925	Appointed Chancellor of the Exchequer. Makes bad decision to return Britain to gold standard.
1929– 1939	Remains Member of Parliament but is given no government position. Works as writer and journalist.
1940	Appointed prime minister. Leads Britain's fight against Nazi Germany.
1941	Asks U.S. and Soviet Union to join in fight against Hitler.
1945	His government defeated in General Election. No longer prime minister but remains M.P.
1951	Appointed prime minister again. But now very old and ill.
1955	Resigns as prime minister. Continues writing and painting.
1964	Resigns as Member of Parliament at age 80.
1965	Dies on January 24 at age 90.

anti-Semitic: having a prejudice, or unthinking hostile attitude, against Jews as a religious or ethnic group

armaments: weapons and machinery used to fight wars

blockade: a way of keeping enemies out by a wall or by patrols

cavalry: soldiers who fight on horseback

communist: related to political and economic system in which all land and businesses belong to the state, which manages them on behalf of the people

Conservative Party: British political party with outlook that represents interests of business and landowning classes

constituents: citizens who can elect

Dervish: member of a Muslim fighting force in North Africa and the Middle East

fascist: extreme political opinion that believes the state or a leader should have total control over people's lives

genocidal: wanting to kill all members of an ethnic or racial group

gold standard: an economic policy in which paper money can be exchanged for the same value in real gold

hunger marches: political demonstrations by unemployed workers demanding jobs to earn money to buy food for themselves and their families

Labor Party: British political party holding socialist (see below) views

Liberal Party: British political party with progressive, moderate views

Member of Parliament (M.P.): person elected to represent voters in Britain's law-making assembly (parliament)

Nazi: member of the German National Socialist party, an extreme fascist (see above) group led by Adolf Hitler

revolutionaries: people who want to make political changes, often using violence

right wing: holding capitalist or Conservative (see above) political views

socialist: related to a system or condition of society in which means of production are owned and controlled by the state

TO FIND OUT MORE

BOOKS

Severance, John B. *Winston Churchill: Soldier, Statesman, Artist*. New York: Clarion Books, 1996.

Reynoldson, Fiona. *Winston Churchill* (Leading Lives series). Chicago: Heinemann Library, 2001.

Krull, Kathleen. *V is for Victory: America Remembers World War II*. New York: Knopf, 1995.

INTERNET SITES

Winston Churchill Home Page of the Churchill Center and Societies
www.winstonchurchill.org
A large and comprehensive site. Includes texts from many speeches and a timeline.

Churchill: The Evidence
www.churchill.nls.ac.uk
An Internet exhibition about Churchill's life. Includes photographs and documents.

Winston Churchill Biography
http://gi.grolier.com/wwii/wwii_churchill.html
A concise account of the main events in Churchill's life.

Modern World History: People at War
www.bbc.co.uk/education/modern/people/peoplhtm.htm

Modern World History: Allied Victory
www.bbc.co.uk/education/modern/allied/alliehtm.htm

Bite Size History: The Division of Europe
www.bbc.co.uk/schools/gcsebitesize/history/1945to89/2eastandwestrev2.shtml

The three sites listed above contain background information, photographs, and documents on European politics from the 1930s to the 1950s and about people's lives during World War II.

INDEX

About the Author

Award-winning author **Fiona Macdonald** has written almost two hundred books for young people, mostly on historical topics. Educated at Cambridge University, UK, she was for many years a tutor in medieval history at the University of East Anglia. She has taught groups of adults and school children, and appeared on radio and TV. She now lives in a remote region of highland Scotland, where her ancestors originated, and writes full-time.